LOST HORSE PRESS NEW POETS SERIES

New Poets | Short Books | Volume III

LOST HORSE PRESS NEW POETS SERIES

New Poets | Short Books | Volume III

Series Editor | Marvin Bell

FUGUE | *Emily Bobo*

SHINE TOMORROW | *Joel Craig*

RETURN OF THE FIST | *Amy Lingafelter*

LOST HORSE PRESS
SANDPOINT · IDAHO

ACKNOWLEDGMENTS

Joel Craig:
GutCult: "Thin Red Line" and "High Park"
The City Visible: Chicago Poetry for the New Century (Cracked Slab Books): "Street Dad"
A Public Space: "California Poem"

Amy Lingafelter:
Ninth Letter: "My Cousin" and "Terra Firma"
Satellite Telephone: "The Summer I Started Pickling Things"
Crab Orchard Review: "The Grandmothers"
The Iowa Review: "The Counterfeiter"

FIRST EDITION

Series Editor: Marvin Bell
Cover Art: Atom Welch
Interior and cover design by Christine Holbert.

Emily Bobo photo by Michael Lindsay.
Joel Craig photo by Raymond Craig.
Amy Lingafelter photo by Rebecca Stone.

Library of Congress Cataloging-in-Publication Data

Cash, Gwendolyn, 1968-
  Acts of contrition / Gwendolyn Cash. The owl's ears / Boyd W. Benson. Liminal : a life of cleavage / Lisa Galloway.
      p. cm. — (Lost Horse Press new poets series. New poets, short books)
  ISBN 978-0-9762114-7-1 (alk. paper)
  1. American poetry—21st century. I. Benson, Boyd W., 1961- II. Galloway, Lisa, 1978-
III. Title. IV. Title: Owl's ears. V. Title: Liminal.
  PS617.C37 2007
  811'.608—dc22

                    2006100084

Who best represents American ideals and the American character? We have for eight years suffered a degree of criminality and ineptitude at the national level that could scarcely have been imagined. Our White House and Congress were kidnapped by corrupt capitalism, lunatic imperialism and hypocritical evangelism. They are not patriots who invaded and tortured in our name. They are not patriots who repeatedly broke national and international law. They are not patriots who refuse to pay for education and social services, and to whom neither the common good nor the lives of our children matter.

How in the horrors of the past eight years were Americans able to maintain an inner life force? The inner life needs a soul. Which is to say, culture. Which is to say, the arts.

And is it not the American ideal to create something good not seen before? Reader, here in volume three of *New Poets / Short Books* are three more poets, genuine poets. It is amazing to me, and a great solace in these times, to come across poets who do not make a career of telling others what art is, but who simply push the envelope to express what matters, and whose writing, given your open attention, will be, like they say, money in your pocket.

Why take art as it comes? Because nothing better illustrates the American character than the individualism inherent in art. Crucially, the best poetry does not succumb to a dumbing-down in the search for a wider audience, nor do business with those prosaic village explainers who keep telling us what it is. It does not need professors or theorists.

The lunatics and hacks that made up our national government for eight years could not keep Americans from singing and dancing, from imagining and pretending, or from making art in numberless ways. And they could not make poetry small. For the poets of any age are not only of their time. They hold hands with the poets of ancient times and of all time since. Poets and other artists have kept alive the life force of nations when it was hidden from the rest of the world. Let it be so again.

This 3-in-1 series is meant to give voice to a range of poets who have yet to publish a book and have generally gone about their writing in private. It will publish poets who are very much in the game but not in the network. Hence, it will not be run as a contest, nor will it accept submissions. The idea is indebted to *Poets of Today*, the Scribner series edited by John Hall Wheelock from 1954 to 1962, which published in eight volumes first books by twenty-four poets, three poets at a time under a single cover.

—M.B., July 4, 2008

TABLE OF CONTENTS

RETURN OF THE FIST | *Amy Lingafelter*

FUGUE

poems | EMILY BOBO

My father was born in a boxcar and built his house one hundred feet from the tracks because he couldn't sleep without the night train's stampede. My mother was born in a farmhouse and built her ranch on Grandfather's land. Blindfold, twirl and release her, and she will point north every time. Born in 1977 in rural Kansas, I live and write in Bloomington, Indiana, with my husband, marimbist and composer, Kevin Bobo. A recovering musician myself, I quit the piano after sixteen years of study, but it was many years after that before I was able to realize why. I always write to figure out the "why." Mirrors and loved ones often lie. The page does not.

—*Emily Bobo*

Fugue / fyoog
Noun

1. *Music:* Type of contrapuntal comp. for particular no. of parts or 'voices' (described thus whether vocal or instr., e.g. fugue in 4 parts, fugue in 3 vv.). The point of fugue is that the vv. enter successively in imitation of each other, the 1st v. entering with a short melody or phrase known as the Subject (different from sonata-form 'subject' in that it is merely melodic and short). When all the vv. have entered, the *Exposition* is over. Then (normally) there comes an *Episode* or passage of connective tissue (usually a development of something that has appeared in the exposition) leading to another entry or series of entries of the *Subject,* and so on until the end of the piece, entries and episodes alternating. (*The Oxford Dictionary of Music*)

2. *Psychiatry:* [A] pathological condition describing vacillating states of amnesia and total recall. [. . . .] A fugue state is related to both hysteria and dissociation. Unlike them, however, and distinct from 'common' psychogenic amnesia, fugue states are always characterized by a flight from usual surroundings, the mind becoming a virtual tabula rasa except for basic functions and general knowledge. [. . . . T]hus fugue represents a flight in two senses: an escape from one mode of consciousness to another, to a new or unfamiliar place [,] the primary condition of [a] fugue [being] internal and external flight from self, from home. (Robert W. Rudnicki, *Percyscapes: The Fugue State in Twentieth-Century Southern Fiction*)

about piano, to prove how over-it she was;
then a friend invited her to his concert, and
she was the embarrassed audience, the educated
one, who didn't shout "Bravo!" and rush the stage
with teddy bears and wrapped, red flowers—
Chopin didn't pause in those places—so
she didn't nod in agreement with the belted,
short-sleeve-shoulder-pad dresses who said, "He's got
the touch." Then, smug and superior, sunning
herself on the side of the River Ego, her dam,
marked "precious," burst, and Ms. Woods'
"She's got it" and her mother's "God's gift" rushed out,
carrying away all her pretty, potted roses.

PIANO LETTERS

I

I waited for you—and I wait for you—my voice, my mute,
   my amp, my heart.

When you touched me, made love to me with your hands,
   your pain in my mouth,
I would bare my strings, let you beat me with felt-tipped hammers,
   each stroke an invitation to sing, each quivering string
   a resounding "yes" and "again."

And O, how you told me things with those hands!
It was in the way you reached for me, all my black keys,
   your fingers flat and worried against my ivory,
   fingerprinting dream inside me.

I would sing for you what you could not, what your chords would not
   produce for you, I did. I do.
And who else will understand this need to suffer into singing? this
   need for pain, for bleeding, for this ritual un-naming of feeling?
I wait for you—I wait—my voice-gone, my mute, my amputated,
   my vibrating, heart.

THE RECOVERING MUSICIAN AND
THE PARABLE OF THE MUSTARD SEED

(Matthew 13:31-32)

Her mother told her another parable:
The kingdom of heaven is like a daughter,
        which a single mom bore and enrolled
        in piano lessons.
Though the daughter was the smallest mother-
        seed, the Mother hoped, when she grew,
        she would be the most appropriately
        charming and become Miss America,
        or Mrs. Somebody-Important at least,
        so that all of the other mothers could
        reside in the glory of the Mother.

II

You never touch me, sit with me, play me, anymore.
A cappella? Baby, you never could hold a pitch.

And what no one ever told you about Billie, about Trane,
        there's a limit to sound: Billie birthed it, Trane
        breathed it, you simply beat it, out of me.

But you should know, baby, these keys still hum,
        with or without you.

And I am the drug, the addiction.
I am your dying.
A music, a voice, a sound so dissonant,
        so possessible, you forget your own,
        you forget how to speak.

I am the rival, the life-giver, the one you turn to
        to know you.
You forget yourself, I learn you so well.
And I would cut out your tongue,
        if it meant you would not leave me.
But you have already cut off your thumbs.

And would that I could bleed, I should. After all you bled
        on me.
Your blood fed me. Led me to song.

It was your heartache you gave me.
And I devoured it, came to your heart, so worn and gnawed,
    so close to ache, I ate that, too.

DEAR PIANO,

Mother has said that I can play with you today.
Mother has said that I must play with you until dinner.
Mother has said that we can play "Gavotte."
We cannot play "scales," the game we do not know the end to.
We cannot play "Tarantella," for we cannot play randomly with abandon.
Mother has said that we can play "Goldfish."
Mother has said that we must play softly, for Brother is home.
Brother does not like to hear us play.
Brother has said he wants to break our ivory teeth.
So let us pretend we are gold-colored fish in dark water.
Let us not play anything which will betray our anger.
Let us pretend not to have the power.

She never had one, though she had thousands.
She used them to record the Recovering Musician's lessons
    and pretended not to notice the evidence, the erasures:
    all that missing Haydn and Bach.
She did not ask about the picture the Recovering Musician stole,
    that one of her smiling.
She did not know the Recovering Musician framed it in pink plastic
    flowers and would hide it in a green artillery lockbox after the funeral.
She bought only pastel pencils and vased them in cups, great
    wooden bouquets in mugs on nightstands and kitchen chairs.
Each one becomes a love song, a variation on Ruth.

THE RECOVERING MUSICIAN QUIT
THE PIANO BECAUSE

I

Her mother liked to ask her to play for people at dinner parties.
Her mother liked to tell people her daughter played the piano, that
    God had given her the "gift."

II

Her father never came to her recitals.
At her first recital, the bench was too high, and her feet couldn't reach
    the pedals.
For recitals she had to memorize music. Sometimes, when she was
    nervous, when her feet couldn't find the pedals, her memory
    would leave her, like her father, and though she could feel the
    music's absence, the space around where it should be, she
    couldn't remember its beginning, its middle, or its ending.

III

Ruth died.

IV

Her mother disowned her and forbid her the use of her piano. It was
    a Mason and Hamlin tuned to melancholy and rage, heavy on
    the bass and light on the treble.

She had to practice piano in churches and recital halls, on electronic
keyboards and uprights.

She didn't like playing piano in churches. There was never any
privacy, too much God hanging around: God dying on the
windows, on the walls; God suspended from the ceiling and the altar.

She didn't like playing piano in recital halls. The hush felt too sacred,
too close, too familiar, and silence lived just outside the
spotlight, where memory could not illuminate the music she
was playing or the faces she recognized as human.

She didn't like playing her portable electronic keyboard. The notes
were too separate. The sound was disjointed, like her
emotions after snorting cocaine.

And she didn't like playing uprights. Her mother had had one. Its
hammers' felt had been chewed away by the mouse that lived
inside it. When she practiced, the mouse would run back and
forth along the sound board, scampering along the strings. It
became a game where she would try to hit it, to feel the slight
give, to hear the thick, dull thud replacing the expected note.

V

At college her new teacher never smiled the way Ruth had.

Her new teacher never taught lessons from the hospital bed in his
living room, wearing a fuchsia nightgown, his whole body
lifting and falling to the beat of "Gollywog's Cake Walk." He
never scheduled her lesson last so they could go as late as
they wanted, never suggested they blow off their studies to go
to Love's café for cheeseburgers, never knew how to turn her
around, asking, "Why not you?"

He always charged her for extra lessons and never assigned her
music that required both hands, both registers, heart and body.

Her new teacher assigned only Bach.

She never got Bach right. She couldn't play Bach angry. She
couldn't play Bach sad. These were the two ways she knew
how to play.
Once, right after Ruth died, she had made an entire room weep. For
that she used her grief.
Ruth had said she played with balls. For that she used her anger.
For a while, after Ruth died, her anger disappeared into a bottle, a
pipe, a straw. Then her anger started to appear uninvited.
Her anger started to attack her. It liked to eat her fingers.
She started head-butting the piano to shut up the anger.
She broke the metal rod that connects the pedals to the piano,
snapped it in half because the anger felt like a fire spreading
up her legs.

VI

Her mother stopped asking her to play for people at parties.
Her mother stopped telling people her daughter played the piano.
Her mother reminded her that Lucifer was a musician before he fell.
The other students started staring into her practice room, tiny faces
filling up her window, number eight in a row of twelve in a hall
lined with teeny, square-windowed rooms stuffed with baby pianos.
They stared at her anger.
She started punching the piano. She did it because she couldn't get
it right, couldn't make her fingers feel anything but anger or
grief, couldn't make a dead woman smile or an old man love her.

VII

She acquired a lover, a musician, a virtuoso, the Chopin of the
marimba. And he was kind and good like Ruth had been kind
and good, but she couldn't play for her lover, couldn't let him

see her, not inside her, because her anger wouldn't let her.

And she became convinced that being in love meant being inside
someone else, meant being happy and that being happy
meant not being angry, and that playing the piano meant being
sad, meant being lonely, meant being left with no memory on
a dark stage where her feet couldn't reach the pedals.

So she used her anger to collapse her sound board, to snap it in half,
to unwind each of the three strings for each of her eighty-eight
keys, to peel the felt from each wooden hammer with her
teeth. She stroked her anger with her grief two hundred
sixty-four times, saying, "Goodbye, Ruth." She opened the
little window in her door and shoved the piano through in
splintered pieces.

And this is where she lives: in her square room with her lover, broken
piano filling the window, marimba filling the room.

See, how she waits for his expected note to replace the dull, thick
thudding of her heart?

See, how happy replaces the piano?

III

And what do you think? You think he can make you sing?
Think he can mourn you, rage you, re-create you for you
        when you've forgotten yourself and me and everything
        that makes you me?
Think he'll let you lay hands on him the way I let you me?

Will he love your insolent beating? your incessant cheating?
Will he stand for days of silence? for a dampening of dynamics,
        for overwrought diction, forced notation and one-sided
        conversation?

Will he be able to support your sporadic attention? your
        compulsive addiction to sound, to expression, to
        weeping and screaming, to loving and bleeding?
Will he understand the swooning, the blackouts, the
        channeling of ear and body and God and oneness?

Ruth had said the Recovering Musician's hands looked like hers.

Before the spots, the creases, the gnarliness set in.

Small hands. Strong hands. Pretty hands.

Blue-collar-washer-woman/welder hands: short, powerful fingers on broad palms.

Gentle, maker hands.

Hands the Recovering Musician cherished because Ruth had loved them.

Hands the Recovering Musician peeled and ate because Ruth had loved them.

Hands the Recovering Musician buried in silence, after she'd consumed all the music
Ruth had left her.

THE PARABLE OF THE WEEDS, AS EXPLAINED TO THE RECOVERING MUSICIAN *(Matthew 13:36-43)*

The one who sowed the good daughter is me, the Mother.
The field is the piano, and the good daughter stands for the Mother.
The bad daughter is the daughter of the Father, and the Father is
    Satan incarnate; the Father is the enemy.
The harvest is the piano recital, and the harvesters are those who
    congratulate me, the Mother, on how hard my good daughter
    practiced, how well she performed, how pretty and small her
    dress made her look in the lime-light.
The weeds are the spirits of rebellion, fostered by the Father and the
    radio; they must be exorcised.
I, the Mother, will send out my power, my love, to weed the daughter
    of all sprigs of independence, creativity, and ego.
These weeds take the form of burnable materials: shorts worn under
    mandatory skirts, two-piece swimsuits, alternative music,
    books without pictures, and all other forms of paper secrets.
These weeds will be flushed, pitched, burnt, or ripped into finger-
    sized strips for eating.
This will cause weeping and gnashing of teeth.
Then the good daughter will again be pretty and belong to the Mother.
She who has ears, let her hear.

IV

In my dreams still I am you
my strings your chords my keys
your teeth my hammers your
lips my pedals your tongue I
play you tune ballooning
belly swelling mouth drumming
tongue against teeth exploding no
imploding you I swallowed your
words consumed my hands bound
my feet banned you days my
nights belong to you anyway

How I stalk myself
with you—memory's
constructions of
you—like a scent
its object, a mouth
its breath, a word
its tongue, a hammer
its string; like a note
its pitch and a belly
its feet. You are
only me. Yours
is the lid I cannot
let close, the wound
I tend with salt
and carefully.

THE PIANO CLOSET:
EULOGY FOR THE PIANO TEACHER

Ruth in the thumb-frayed edges of the wrong piece
  of music, in the dust let loose from its pages,
   in the scores of scores not-quite-the-right-one
   stuffed into all reachable space.
Ruth in the haphazard hierarchy of genius: Glover
  next to Schumann over Bach below Gillock.
Ruth in the clover footstool for reaching the unreachable.
Ruth in the hanging mirror on the face of an open door.
Ruth in the easy closeness of overstuffed space.
Ruth in the pull-chain bulb: functional, essential, light
  minus glare and diffusion.
Ruth in the silence, in the stillness of notes
  waiting.

CODA: "ACCORD FINAL"

The "Accord Final"
is a sculpture by Arman,
a Franco-American artist,
of a busted and bronzed
baby grand piano.

It was as if Arman had known how it would end for them,
    the RM and her piano, known it the way ancient
    Greeks had known the secret bodies of stones;
    perhaps he started it the day of their first recital.
He would have begun tentatively, a mortician arranging
    his corpse: he folded the sound board carefully,
    embalmed its legs with uncrumpable metal, crossed
    its strings, de-felted hammers nine and ten, not twelve,
    and then he nailed its body to a cement stage, nailed
    it in the permanent shadow of the performance hall.
But something in its ordered creases disappointed even
    a dandelion spore searching for some silt-filled
    pocket or knot of string, some tangled dysfunction
    to hold onto or lose itself in.

SHINE TOMORROW

poems | JOEL CRAIG

I was born in Des Moines, Iowa, in 1971. In 1974 I sat with my sister under an oak library table while a tornado flattened our neighbor's house — my earliest memory. For the past eleven years I've made my home in Chicago, working variously as a deejay, graphic designer and art director. My first experience with learning an artistic process was in chorus. Singing eight and twelve-part harmonies taught me to hear in a way that has greatly informed how I write poetry. It's in my poetic blood to make disjunctive arrangements. I like how I think when I'm making a poem. If a poem starts breathing for itself, my role becomes that of steward. Otherwise I'm merely pressing words into service.

—Joel Craig

God damn it, you've got to be kind.
                                    — *Kurt Vonnegut*

This war cannot be won.
The memory of the garden illusion caught me up
again in the turmoil, viewing my inner self
as an old person looking at distant scenery.
Add whenever the owner was asked to put on a demonstration.
When he gave the mule his first command.
Add the badly painted back-drop. Plus
my gaze to the left. It is not a good place to be,
to follow any verbal order you're given.
First you have to get my attention. Someone
somewhere is trying to get my attention.
The query came from somewhere inside me, quite gracefully.
Add tired. Tired, tired. Plus decide
what such-and-such really is. Add effective
tools in the war against so monstrous a wrong.
Add ideology superimposed on us during the course of our learning.
Add the maverick must be allowed to retreat
to his private domain and live in any manner
he finds rewarding. Add interminable
conversations with your cats. Plus
watching television all day long. Plus as long
as we don't interfere with the freedom
or well-being of any other person.
Plus easier enforcement will catch more criminals.
Plus the international politics of debt.
Add a lot of what I've been talking about

has to do with the "other guy." Add more and more
companies are requiring pre-employment urine testing.
Not just bus drivers and firemen, add furniture salesmen.
Grocery store clerks. Add recipients of public housing,
university loans, or academic grants. Add veteran cops.
Add the daily
shaving of the head and body. Today verbal assurance
is acceptable, but what about tomorrow. Add tomorrow.
Add what extent do you feel it is justifiable
for someone else to control your personal behavior
if it contributes to the public benefit?
Add I have questions in one pocket & secrets in the other.
Add I've got nothing to hide.
To this delicious feeling of being alive add definition
of a police state, were it to quietly materialize around you.
Plus proportions of any serious effort to help those
with debilitating mental illnesses. Add children
who have no families, no food,
no education and no hope.
Plus interactive software.
Add we're a drag strip.
Remodeling experts.
Add redneck gangs with names like the "Spookhunters."
Add panicky local authority.
Subtract modernism.
Add propaganda. Reasonable suspicion. Swift action.
If you are a person in authority,
you now don't have to confront the suspected wrongdoer;
you confront their possessions instead.
Add quick-witted reporters.
Add legislature. Boot camps.
To "six pack" stucco tenements add weed & seed urban rescue.
Weary populations preoccupied with fantasies of becoming Byzantium.

Electrified teenagers of all classes.
Deceptive technology.
Add your personal limits.
Add our parents' permission.
The social burden of servicing the deficit.
Add comment.
I had a horrible nightmare
last night, far more intense than any dream I've had in years.
Add I was at a hotel. Add everything I owned was in the room.
Plus I'm naked.
This wonderful glow inside my being—
the expanse of green grass and the shimmering
leaves vibrating in the sunlight
making this a wonderful place
to sit and contemplate. Here is what happened.

(for Greg Purcell)

STREET DAD

Let me try to lay out what I think I understand
                          about my life. I took a sip
                          of wine and plunged.

The new plague has worked so quickly we've returned
                          nearly to equilibrium.

What's behind me has been built out of nothing
                          into a whole row of apartments
                          full of exotic people.

You can presume relative safety. I'm a quiet person.
                          I don't make a lot of noise
                          in public.

The most I can ever do is establish what appears to be
                          a relatively safe level
                          for myself, for my own body and mind.

A flash of amusement, realizing the invitation
                          to pounce could be taken
                          more than one way.

I have two cats who live outside hunting gophers and mice.
                          There's a bit more to climb
                          before we level out.

He was thin, shy and tended to be exacting and impatient,
                          but I was a good, caring father.

He had the heart and clearness of mind
                    to be a therapist. We could afford
                    little in the way of school.

Emptying his pockets we came across
                    a policy for trying out
                    new groups of people.

A safe level for particular bodies, nervous systems
                    and private individuals with questions.

They may be a bit uncomfortable about what
                    they think I'm doing
                    but they've no reason to stop me.

I used to have a dog called Bruno
                    but when he died I didn't
                    have the heart to replace him.

I learned what it was to be really poor, what it does
                    to the human spirit.

Fundamental things still apply—
                    a greenness that makes Ireland
                    look grey encircling a perfect crescent bay.

A place in which only self-deluded, naïve people hope
                    for things to get better. Las Vegas
                    and the end of western history.

Above all is the ghost of sunk capital. Terrible assets
                    that won't be born. Telling a cop
                  to fuck off.

It's a strange feeling to look up the hill, across the grass, and see
                    those buildings staring down
                    where there used to be nothing but sky and trees.

She never really said anything I could count on, and I didn't want to
                    waste any more time or energy than I had to
                    on people who play games.

So to you, yes. Yes for telling the truth. To your intuitive fingers
                    and all the rest of you, what are you
                    trying to say?

She'll be coming to be with me for a while. I'm meeting her plane
                    tomorrow morning.

She's wonderfully gentle. Down the stairs into the living room, the fire
                    is still throwing off occasional sparks.

Lit fingertips move thoughtfully
                    up over the top of my shoulder
                    and pause behind my ear.

Do cities decay differently in the New World?
                    There's a faint touch of tease here—biological
                    warfare sort of stuff. Recreation crisis.

Looking comfortably at ease with private images.
                    Keep silent in deference to the possibly
                    imminent end of the human race.

Of course there are different ways to terrorize
                    from the sky. If he's the kind
                    that gets easily irritated, I'll likely find out.

Evolution rapidly manufactures new species or subspecies
                    out of their domesticates.

I didn't know I was suffering from an illness
                    known as depression. For the first time
                    in my life, I thought I was seeing the world.

I sat for a moment, staring at my knees as I tried
                    to put broad, wide images
                    into small, tidy words.

THIN RED LINE

After giving birth, she says, she dismissed the universe
    and told it that it was
    on its own.

Without my presence there will be no magic in your life.

Pretty intense, but okay.

Sometimes when you go through a miserable thing
    you become allergic to everyone.

The nurturing mother reaches for her child's hand,
    feeling with pleasure the texture of the skin
    and the solid bones of the fingers.

She takes the grossest materials and blows them
    into shimmering bubbles.

So we rejoice in the salvage. The afternoon and evening clouds
    through the window at a specific moment.

As long as you stay off the piano keys.

And the me who thought I knew who I was woke up
    by the oyster bar.

He has no conscience because he has no need
    of humility in his life. Somewhere, out there
    in the shifting sands of Death Valley
    is a nothing to repeat always —

Composed harmonies can be claustrophobic at first.
        My recollection of the endless summer
        is almost unbearable.

Tension between perception of reality and growing up
        mesmerized me and my friends.

With the mirage of unattainable futures in the distance
        it became urgent to wring as much
        freedom from the night as possible.

Just a few minutes ago, I was looking out the living room window
        and two dogs were playing
        on the boulevard.

Actually I had a wonderful time. The only horse I bet on
        was a winner despite narrow odds.

And it's just so fun to speculate, to play a role
        in making a nature scene.

When the rival withdrew from the field
        their faces showed confusion
        or something like embarrassment.

Taking pleasure to strut around with a gun in your belt.

And it's just so fun to speculate —

In the kitchen, a soup was simmering on the stove.
        On the tile counter were green lettuces and bright-
        red tomatoes heaped into piles alongside loaves of bread.

I went through a few moments of seeing my worst faults.

Ceiling high bookcases thrust into the room.

There was a central room, surrounded by a veranda
                sloping downwards, outwards on all sides.

Of course it's not unthinkable that I've held several hands and waited
                to cry and never cried but wanted to
                but was filled with too much anxiety.

You're not obvious for saying it's dark & intolerable
                outside. It's a soggy grey fucker

giving dignity and purpose to small rebellions—
                the monotonous hot-rod and beach
                riots and motherly perspective.

What is really happening in the brain is happening
        in darkness.

It's theater time. My tinnitus is really out there
        and there is no way of getting away from it.

After the letter-reading was over, she asked me
        if I would like to come out to the farm after work
        on Friday, to stay the weekend.

Something was taking shape across the room. There was a sense
        of gold somewhere in the red. The legs
        of the red-painted kitchen table glowed,
        and the room was alive with a soft light.

Twenty-four hours later I was talking again, sitting
        on his brown leather couch, keeping silent
        while he did things to his tape-recorder
        on the low table in front of me.

It's a sort of brother relationship—the brother neither of us had.

I didn't talk about my reason for being there. The flowers
        were shimmering. The flowers on the curtain
        were shimmering and we're holding hands
        for the last time.

Walking up the street at midnight we approached a frail grandmother
        who was pulling her grocery cart behind her,
        talking on a cellular phone.

To be too thorough or specific about sensing possible let-downs
        in a possible romance is to establish
        a place for them in the subconscious mind.

We walked past a recommended Portuguese restaurant.
        All attempts at smiling or sounding lighthearted
        had been abandoned.

The continuation of the human species itself
        obviously requires we get to work
        very quickly.

The dimension behind the dizziness. Boy, I really felt that drink!
        I may be sloppy, but let me explore the sexual. Wow.
        I may be spacey in the head, but my body
        knows where it's at.

It wasn't until I had reached the hotel, getting out of the cab
        that I remembered the blue nightgown, and laughed.

The door opened and a mass of electrified silver hair poked itself
        into my field of vision. Words carving through my mind
        occasionally taking a wrong turn
        through labyrinthine caverns.

I didn't even know I wanted cornbread with scallions until now.

Not be too thorough or specific about sensing possible let-downs,
        but you told me it would be a wonderful experience.

Her bluff is being called. The clouds are beginning to lift.
        The sun is breaking through.

I sat on the couch for a long time, mentally replaying the conversation,
        word by extraordinary word.

In the early evening, we gathered together for supper.

She didn't talk about my reason for being there.
                There used to be no limits
                but now the State is with us continually.

He's a person, who, when he's attracted to someone
                intuitively senses what's lacking in
                their emotional life. A compulsion
                to become whatever they need most.

A few words are needed here regarding
                the neurotransmitter serotonin. I don't excuse
                the boredom. I want the boredom.

It wasn't very crowded, probably because of the rain,
                but there were some patient, raincoated visitors
                who were obviously used to this kind of weather.

It is in the head I am attentive.

I follow the unfolding of an inner experience
                sculptured with moss-covered stone
                and moving water. Subtle gradations of color in the pebbles.

Imagine a scientific expedition to a distant world. The continuation
                of the human species itself
                obviously requires we get to work.

Novel structures indicate novel processes.

The sight of the great seated Buddha on the path
                above the garden pierces my heart.

CALIFORNIA POEM

What is needed is a recognizable molecule that carries the unstable
        promise to the brain. A good-humored Buddha
        area of the self.

I've tried and tried but it keeps slipping away. We stopped
        at a spot overlooking the bay
        at the same time both observing and performing.

After the patrolman followed us we joked about dodging a bullet,
        the first stirrings of pleasant feelings evident
        without introspective urges.

Afterward, sleeping was tricky but it worked out okay.
        I said thank you but I have to go
        on with the rest of my life.

It's simple, I think. I open my mouth to say just that, but everyone
        says something along these lines,
        seeing places and things with their eyes closed.

A clear vision of big cities as actors in their own right.
        When I close my eyes the first stirrings of
        pleasant feelings become evident.

I rise and lead the way through the kitchen and dining room
        and down the hallway to the bedroom
        feeling solidly connected to the physical world.

A good humored Buddha area of the self. I spend the night
          on a pad in their bedroom, for once
          tired by the music, the air clean and cool.

The piano plays on, undeterred, and in my place on the floor
          I imagine my preferred self-image
          awakening to clinical sunshine.

It's yet another distraction. How fast do you hold to yourself,
          saying tiresome truths over and over again
          to the tired people who rush into your life.

Have you ever been to Death Valley? I've wanted to see it for years
          but haven't yet had the chance.
          There are personalities you never forget.

We packed the car with sandwiches and the makings of a good salad.
          The idea appealed to everyone.
          For the first time I missed the road.

At the entrance a small sign nailed to a telephone pole announced,
          fresh oysters for sale, as if I'd built
          an imaginary destination in my mind.

What will operate against a swift frame is a certain coolness in the work.
          When we walked into the living room
          my chest tightened, though I knew what to expect.

So far it wasn't at all like my fantasy. The kitchen was comfortably large,
          with a linoleum floor so old its original pattern
          was lost in a general brown-ness.

He led me down the hall and out the back door. We walked along
            a narrow dirt path, past clumps of early narcissus,
            under buckeye and pine trees.

One scene in particular stays with me. The hero has wandered
            into a valley where he sees, all around him
            plants thrusting up by the tens of thousands.

For most of my life, whenever I was being introduced to a roomful
            of people I didn't know, the tiny muscles on either side
            of my mouth would go into a twitching spasm

if I tried to maintain a smile. Noise erupted around the table.
            Names of people and places I didn't recognize
            were flying everywhere. Outside was the green world.

RETURN OF THE FIST

poems | AMY LINGAFELTER

I'm a librarian. Generally, I like helping people find things. I'm actually a school librarian, so I really like helping students find things they will enjoy reading. I'm not sure if my helpful nature informs my poetry. Some of the poems I write are distinctively unhelpful, though full of heart, like the right fielder on a Little League team. I am confident that I mean what I write. I was born in July of 1976, so I'm 200 years younger than my country. I'm from Joliet, Illinois, and I'm an extremely helpful person most of the time.

—*Amy Lingafelter*

Much was written about sex.
Hours were spent next to a slow-moving river
which sometimes didn't move at all.
Someone wore something unfortunate.
An animal clung to its mother,
and Mexico emerged in the distance.
The world became more of a place
for largesse, for settling up or down,
for growing out or up,
for being born in the whitest hottest
white hot part of a blow torch,
which would hurt but an instant.
The sound on the TV was turned way down,
and love was made out of town,
and New York City became both a painted scene
and a scene within a scene.
Girls were offered a Refrigerator Mother Theory
that began with Judy and ended with Liza.
There were butterflies and silver flowers,
and love was made out of a holiday weekend and two phone calls.
The East met the West on its own terms, wordlessly and in a bar.
There were fireworks of all sorts.
Children were endlessly entertained
by calling cars, women, names, and faces.
On Lincoln Ave., someone ran over a stray cat,
and a star was totally born.

"Remember" is not the opposite of "forget."
Here, next to the new bananas,
all, uh, flutter,
and attempting to seem benign.
Check out my chicken wings.
Check out my butterfly, social,
my pupils, dilated.
I feel silly, and I, becoming,
fast as a barge under the bridge
to say goodbye to this water,
cannibal and criminal,
flyweight.

It's my chicken wings.
It's Mike T. in his boxer briefs,
photographed getting high
on a beach in Hawaii
with a bunch of surfer kids,
a gaggle of girls
bet their friends a pretty penny,
a black bikini,
that Mike would let them nibble on his ear.
My eyeteeth,

and Mike could seem oblivious
under a headline reading *Maui Wowie.*
Not like keeping pigeons anymore, is it?
It was March. Month of bare and black trees,
the whole world looks like a movie
about high school basketball.

Cold and birdy and gray — barge-like.
So we know this gray, gray walk
like the back of our hand,
fistful of migration.

The running theory on you
is we should've kept you the animal you were,
instead of allowing the animal you've become.
What a treat you were to unleash
in $20 shoes, no socks, white towel.
They could've built Stonehenge
right there in the middle of Brooklyn,
a testament to fierce regularity.
A new banana, the spring equinox,
the day the daylight lasts longer.

We don't need no signs to tell us
what's bound to happen —
and still "remember" is not the opposite of "forget."
It's just ducky on the pond,
my chicken wings, pokey,
my body, a sacred ibis.
I only peck and nibble,
let everything rot.
I called my sister to rescue me,
only once or twice.
I should've told her to tie a message
'round my chicken legs,
set me flying east
to stay with my old Italian corner.
Coach and me, we would eat
everything.

I have been ancient,
a little fancy,
tarred and feathered,
a flying rat or rotten fruit.
I have thrown things
I never wanted to see again
in this water, but nothing sinks.
Gull-like, I have fished them back out again.

Kind of like Mike
(and his limo driver, Jo Jo),
I sat catatonic in the backseat.
And there's lots I don't remember about it.
But more often than not,
regularly,
I made the driver turn around
at the corner and take me back.
Every morning, the sun would rise earlier,
the pigeons let loose on the sky.
Bobbing and weaving,
we still return to the fist.

People on the long road to Recovery
should not attend parties
to hang on the smoking porch.
Depending on the party and who's at the party,
people on the long road to Recovery
should rarely hang out and watch how much they drink,
should bring their exes or books,
should shoot the shit in the corner while using
what they typically use,
a mop, a phone, a condom, in the room
of slight tragedy, of big ego, of age before beauty,
a rager, a stander, a mirror
in the bathroom of the party.
People, on the long road to Recovery,
do not allow photographs of yourselves to be taken!
Because looking at them
later will cause a relapse of enormous proportions,
with various cities visited, two large-ish bottles of rum,
bayonets, museums, the horror, the horror
of just looking at them.
There should be no beating
yourselves up, people,
no expecting miracles when everything is a miracle,
a supreme festivity, summer school.
There should be no wishing at all,
people, for you'll never always be wanting
just one thing.
People who find themselves jonesing
must make most of their meals from the can.

People, don't you want to run
full on after the rabbit in the yard?
Legs flailing, there should be no changing of routines,
for people on the long road to Recovery
should realize what routine means.

I wish I had a cousin like Mercutio
or Johnny Cash.
My cousin was kicked in the face by a horse,
pregnant, indoctrinated, working at the Dollar Store,
in the Air Force, naked behind a shrub,
pregnant, married for three weeks,
when all of a sudden, she evaporated into a POOF! of tiny spores,
she rode the wind southeast,
searching for the right conditions under a tree, a large stone,
to mold on, groove on, get kicked in the face by a horse,
pregnant, promoted and given a key,
felt up by a doctor, pregnant,
which proves once and for all
that there is no extra-spatial deity,
and that actually, not everything costs a dollar.

I started with this poem
and pigs' feet
and preservation
and pickles—
I pickled pickles,
for pete's sake.
A dairy farm.
A ham hock.
Rotgut.
Eggs.

♦

So this is my muscle atrophied—
I sing it like a doo-wop group,
(*trazadone, trazadone, oh traza-trazadone*).
I sing everything like a doo-wop group
on a radio station in the background
at home. Away from home. Far away from home.
Can you hear me through brunch and dust?
That I could love to be innocuous,
I would've never started pickling.
The summer I started pickling things,
I started thinking: some *thing*
mattered once.
A thing, a thing, a thing,
pickled.

♦

Some things are innocuous,
and some things are for show,
and some things are necessarily showy,
but most things are innocuous.

♦

And then there's us,
during the summer I started pickling things,
I rode a horse,
which, I found out,
though I should've known,
if done right,
is like every other thing
that requires my body.
It's like trying to control a horse.
It's like trying to control my body.
Don't you ever feel like you never know what you'll do next?

♦

I started pickling things.
I started knowing which things to pickle.
And I won't lie, at first, there were vegetables . . .
disguised as people . . .
disguised as themselves!

I built
a huge vat
and pickled *two* cars.
One was a Volkswagen.
I pickled my brothers.
I pickled eels.
Until then, I was unaware
that eels even live in America.
Eels are here.
I pickled my biology textbook
from freshman year,
I pickled arrest records of past lovers,
I pickled my cell phone,
which had been pickled once before,
but pickling it reminded me
how tricky time can be.
I pickled, no lie, a mirror.
I pickled headlines
from important days—
Pickling of Things Begins Today,
the 31st of May.
I pickled three generations
of ancestors, not mine.
I pickled household items
and family heirlooms—
boy, it's a long life I've lived
to have pickled so many things.
And then (not to brag)
I started
to get
exotic:
Shame!
I pickled Shame.

And Youthfulness.
And what they call Horse Sense,
just to prove that I had it.
And two times, Complete Indifference.
And, attempted once:
Confidence.
I can't claim
to have pickled
the whole shebang—
it pains me to say,
some things
just don't need
pickling.

MONOTREMATA

Eggless! Swimmer-y!
Made-up for tomfoolery,
my transparency should be
less about science
and more about me,

and hairless and eggless,
swimmer-y, and shimmer-y, legless,
to waterworks, to evil,
to big guns and a baby,
me in a swimsuit
in front of a family,

and I'm a rock,
and it's a rock
they put under my bed
to encourage fertility,
my legs, my legs
don't need encouraging,
a dirty rock dug up,
a clean rock from a stream,
a needle, some string,
and a nude photo of me,
too tan, too transparent,
too hard to see,
too hairless, too evil,
not at all obscene

the way I thought it would be,
my time

with the eggs
has been lovely
and eggless,
it goes swimmingly,
they will hatch,
I will hatch,
and it'll be all you can see,

a cute uncouth baby
pecks its way
from an egg
while I was out swimming,

telling
a tell-all story
about how I grew a beak
and how I came to be
and how I feel about these things,
complete with dirty jokes and taxidermy,
more dirt,
and wings
that fell off
anciently.

THE GRANDMOTHERS

If you can't accept the fact that
you're human,
then maybe you aren't human.
Take the grandmothers
whose eyelids no longer work,
no longer blink voluntarily,
and who have begun asking for whiskey.
Just because you can ask "How"
doesn't mean you have to ask "How."
And don't think "When"
is what you should be asking either.
Don't think if you ignore this and ask anyway,
and if you happen to get an answer
it will be satisfactory or correct
or satisfactory.
Take the grandmothers,
who have only just begun asking for whiskey,
but who began having babies at 14
in a time when and a place where
they were
neither teenagers,
nor pregnant.
So if you can't accept the fact that
you're human,
then the answers don't matter.
Maybe I am too young to be explaining
the grandmothers, explaining it to the grandmothers,
who cannot swallow, or blink to scoff at the idea.
This fact of listening
means nothing.

Making counterfeit
U.S. dollars,
making love,
making the larkspur
definite are all the things
you can do with a computer
and a little fortitude.

I count half a mil,
you count inches
on my frame,
the little fortitude,
the powerful study.
Well, back it up,
you charming man.
I can count the ways
in which you fail
to back your shit up—
on disk and paper,
with Plan B or numbers,
in words, with deeds.

I count half a mil,
and succeed
in backing you up.
When it's not enough,
we'll make fake.

I only take up five and a half feet,
            though in that space,

I am all that counts,
because of charm.
Because of charm,
I don't think.
Instead,
I bank counterfeit.
I wear nothing
except my socks.

I only succeed in my count.
My smell is larkspur.
My colors are red and purple.
My car and wine are American.
I will be a happy woman
the day I realize
the secret to your charm
is my charm.

> I detect behind
> my neighbor's grin the oncoming bulldozer
> and cannot stop it.
>
> —*James Merrill*

I met my lover at the Ultimate Tan,
the way party goers do cocaine,
the way the palm trees know it's December,
the way you just know
these things are going to happen.
Science. Super String Theory.
Everything is being built.
Beyond the pale,
I drink white zinfandel,
and these thin walls between us are still walls.
Through one,
something told me to fall on my knees,
hear the angel voices,
but I just want a beer.
The little glows that once were
are no more,
and some of us tan nude,
some of us are never nude.
My man and me were made of mud,
he found me and crowned me.
What goes around comes around me,
then it slinks off to separate rooms
with nothing more than winks and nods,

emerges a bronze monster.
Emerges polyethylene, polypropylene.
Emerges: a woman:
can be enticed by beer,
can be enticed by the promise of a better day,
can be enticed by the Earth.
Sod. Oak. Tyvek. Terra *affirma*,
the palm trees droop and rally,
plan accordingly,
and the night is lit up by Equistar,
and I am an anthropologist.
I met my lover at the Ultimate Tan.
Don't listen to me.